# RAW FOOD DIET
# FOR BEGINNERS

The All Natural Way to Lose Weight
Feel Great & Improve your Health

SUSAN ELLERBECK

ISBN-13: 978-1496037893
ISBN-10: 1496037898

# Disclaimer

This information is not intended to provide medical advice or to take the place of medical advice and treatment. Readers are strongly advised to consult a qualified medical professional regarding the treatment of medical conditions. The author and publisher shall not be held liable or responsible for any misunderstanding or misuse of the information contained in this guide or for any loss, damage, or injury caused or alleged to be caused directly or indirectly by any information, treatment, action, or application of any food or food source discussed in this guide. This information is general and is offered with no guarantees on the part of the authors or publisher. This information is not intended to diagnose, treat, cure, or prevent any disease. Nothing in the guide is to be considered personal, legal, or professional advice.

# Table of Contents

# INTRODUCTION

---

Food sustains life, but it is almost unbelievable how many types of food we eat. Most of them, however, are defined by the ways they are prepared and enhanced. We eat foods with geographic descriptions, i.e. "Thai" or "Italian". We eat foods described purely by how they are cooked "barbecue" or "steamed", and we eat foods by various other terms such as "pickled", "kosher", etc.

This book is going to explore something a bit different. In the following pages we'll look at an extremely unique way of eating known as the "raw food" diet. This is not some new dieting technique or a quirky trend, but is a way of life here on Earth for thousands of years.

Raw foods were the very first kinds of foods that human beings could eat. Naturally, they had different types of teeth and jaw structures in the days when raw plants and meats had to be torn apart in order to be eaten, but this established how our bodies worked.

In this guide, we are going to look at "eating" on a step by step basis in order to understand how it works and why unprocessed and uncooked (i.e. raw) foods are the best choices. We will start by looking at those early days of human dietary choices and then explore how modern nutrition is viewed. We will then consider the various methods of eating the raw diet, and even hear what opponents have to say.

In the end, you will walk away with working knowledge of how to use raw foods to your own best advantage, and how to enjoy a whole new type of delicious cuisine!

Let's get started!

# CHAPTER ONE

## Early Eating

In those long ago days usually referred to as the "dawn of time" (or at least as the period of "recorded of human history") we know that there were various types of human-like creatures around. These early people had jawbones that were stronger than our own and teeth that could easily tear apart fibrous plants as well as tough meat.

They also were what we call "hunters and gatherers" and they followed their food throughout the seasons. Whether it was wandering behind herds of animals, or heading away from the frigid winter weather and into more hospitable climates, these were people who did not settle down and raise crops.

These were also not people who enjoyed a vine-ripened tomato in the midst of winter, or any foods that were not immediately on hand. They would eat nuts, tubers, roots, meat, eggs, fish, and any other source that could give them energy and help to keep them alive. Essentially, they ate raw and unprocessed diets.

This means that the nutrients available in the food would have remained unaltered as it went from its natural state and into the human's mouth. For example, the vitamins and essential fatty acids in a fresh nut would be taken in by the body because nothing had been done to unnaturally alter that food.

Many believe that this was, and still is, probably one of the most optimized ways to eat.

Though early human beings' digestive processes would be similar to our own, they would have had to masticate (chew) more and would have had intestinal "flora" entirely different from our own.

## Human Digestion

*Why would they have to chew more?*
*What is intestinal flora?*

In the human body the digestive process doesn't start with food entering the stomach. It begins when the acids from our saliva begin to break down the available carbohydrates in the food. So, digestion starts in the mouth.

Early humans had ALL raw foods, and this would have required that they chew and break things down as much as possible before they could swallow with ease. It would also have been essential to their getting the most nutrition out of their food sources too. Why? Even today, the more you masticate the food (chew it) the more your body can tap into the nutrients immediately in the stomach.

Consider that your saliva and teeth start to break things down, but your taste buds and sense of smell also tell your body which "enzymes" to release in order to break down a food for optimal absorption later in the digestive process. If you smell and then chew food properly, your body intuitively knows how to get the most out of it - particularly when it is raw and unprocessed.

**Enter the Enzymes**

We've just now mentioned enzymes, but this is a huge issue in the raw diet. Human digestive enzymes appear in a few places in the digestive process and include two that are secreted in saliva - salivary amylase and salivary lipase. These break down carbohydrates or fats and prepare foods for further digestion in the stomach.

After chewing, the esophagus forces the food from the mouth and down into the stomach, there a different acid begins to break things down into what are known as amino acids. Additionally, a lot of bacteria are destroyed in the stomach too.

The main event in the stomach is the appearance of pepsin (another enzyme) that works on food to break it apart into protein chains called polypeptides or smaller bits known as peptides or dipeptides. By this time the food should be a sticky liquid that is delivered into the small intestine.

As food passes from the stomach and into the small intestine there are other forces at work, and this is usually when any undigested bits are finally broken down. The liver uses bile from the gall bladder to further break down and use foods, while the pancreas also works to complete the process.

More digestive enzymes come from the fluid in the pancreas, and these are lipase and pancreatic amylase. This is also the part of digestion where disaccharidases appear too.

The goals of these enzymes are alike: to break everything down for absorption into the body. Everything begins to be "absorbed" or metabolized in the small intestine. This is where fat, carbohydrates, and amino acids are taken into the blood stream, and where a lot of native bacteria get to work in further breaking down the foods.

Proteins are the last to go, and they too are the work of the enzymes from the pancreas known as trypsinogen and chymotrypsinogen. They attack the peptide fragments and these are then dissolved by the last of the enzymes, aminopeptidases.

The Results

The results of digestion up until this point are to ensure that carbohydrates, fats, and proteins have been broken down into their useable parts. Namely, into amino acids, monosaccharide (such as glucose), fatty acids, and glycerol.

We haven't mentioned much about the "intestinal flora", but have to at this point. These are considered to be "friendly" bacteria in the intestines and which tend to develop in specific groups over time. They consist mostly of yeasts, fungi, and bacteria that thrive in the intestines and which are responsible for normal functioning.

There are many ways that these can be killed off or destroyed, such as the use of antibiotics on a regular basis. This can actually stop the body from digesting food easily, but early humans would have rarely lost their beneficial bacteria or intestinal flora, and would have enjoyed fairly reliable digestive processes because of it.

One thing you will hear from many advocates of a raw food diet (or those who follow the "primal diet" method) is that this lack of micro-organisms and bacteria has had catastrophic effects on modern humans. They point to the "hygiene hypothesis" that says that exposure to parasites and bacteria strengthen the immune system and prevents allergies. This is something we will definitely explore later, but is worth noting.

So, food is turned into a broken down jelly in the small intestine, and from there it will pass into the large intestine where water is removed from it and everything unusable passes out of the body.

This is a remarkably complicated process, but it is relatively easy to see how the food choices we make can have a major impact on our bodies. If we eat a diet without much nutrition, our body recognizes this and just passes it through the digestive system, taking what little bits it can.

If we alter natural foods, we are automatically reducing their nutrient levels, and this is why so many "raw foodists" advocate eating a diet that is mostly "intact".

## Raw Foods

Intact means uncooked, unprocessed, and even implies organic food. Eating mostly raw, entirely raw, or raw for optimal nutrients means that you are choosing whole food sources based on your nutritional needs. This is a very attentive way to eat because the modern diet tends to overlook balance, nutrition, and intact foods.

Technically, a true raw foodist will say that raw is uncooked and has never reached a temperature higher than 118 degrees Fahrenheit. They will also say it must be unprocessed or even as "wild" as possible, and most say that organic is the way to go because it ensures no irradiation, pesticides, GMO, and/or preservatives.

Is this similar to the standard modern diet? No. Instead, the modern diet includes mostly processed foods that have seen substantial reductions in their nutrient counts. They are seen as much "easier" or convenient in terms of preparing, but they tend to be missing a lot of the benefits of raw foods.

Processed foods are those that have been cooked, milled, dried, irradiated, canned, and managed in a handful of other ways. They are not even close to "whole" foods, and may have been exposed to so much heat and processing by the time they reach you that they are nutritionally void. And quite often they are just plain bad for you.

Yes, some parts of the raw food diet mean chewing your food with greater care in order to facilitate digestion, but that is really the only so-called "glitch". In all other respects, the raw diet can be seen as optimal, but we'll work a bit harder to help you see this for yourself.

In the next chapter we do a sort of side by side comparison of the modern diet and a raw diet. You will see exactly how and why the raw foods are so much better for you.

# CHAPTER TWO

## Modern Foods and Nutrition

You go to the grocery store and you buy only foods that say "whole grain" on the label. You purchase everything in a "low sodium" format to ensure you aren't getting too much salt, and you buy only brands that promise no preservatives and no additives in their foods.

Guess what? You aren't eating naturally, nor are you getting optimal nutrition from the food you choose. While it is great that you are going "whole grain" as much as possible, and avoiding many of the additives and unnecessary flavor enhancers like salt or sugar is wise, you are still purchasing processed foods.

The modern world keeps people pretty far removed from their own food sources and can make it very challenging to understand if you are eating healthily and optimally. Additionally, you are facing the challenges posed by marketers who are trying very hard to sell you the idea of healthy when it is the farthest thing from the truth. Just consider how "healthy" so many types of granola are made to seem when they are usually high in trans or saturated fats, sugars, preservatives, additives, etc.

This is why you have to understand why processed foods are something to avoid. The trick here, however, is coming to understand what that word - processed - really means.

## Processed Foods 101

When a consumer hears the words "processed foods" they tend to envision a can of that orange cheese goop that is sprayed on crackers, or they picture a frozen meal full of pre-made foods that have been sitting in deep freeze for who knows how long. Those are accurate pictures of processed foods, but that same consumer should also envision the following foods when thinking of processed foods too:

- Whole grain cookies;
- All natural canned soups or sauces;
- Dehydrated herbs; and
- High quality fruit juices, among many other foods.

How can such quality food end up on a list of processed items? Easily!

Consider that food processing means:

- Blanched
- Canned
- Condensed
- Cooked
- Dehydrated
- Frozen
- Harvested
- Irradiated
- Milled
- Pasteurized
- Peeled or Trimmed
- Pickled
- Smoked
- Sorted
- Sterilized
- Washed Food processing is not always about taking non-food ingredients and creating some sort of consumable "Frankenfood" (though that is how many processed foods are created - just read the ingredients in Fluff or frozen whipped topping). No, it also should be seen as the standard approach to the modern food supply.

**Hands Off the Food!**

Here is what we mean:

In the not so distant past it was not unusual for people to have gardens that supplied them with many foods. They grew the foods, tended the plants, harvested the foods, and prepared them soon afterward. Often, they might also can or preserve the foods in some ways too.

Today, however, few people ever have a "hands on" experience with any part of the food growth cycle. They don't grow foods, hunt for foods, raise livestock, or even know what part of the world their food might come from. This means that they eat a diet that is processed.

Just consider this brief story:

A family of four heads to the grocery store to get their weekly food supply. While in the produce section they pick up a small box of tasty clementines. They go to the bakery and get two or three fresh loaves of bread, and then they go and buy some fresh fish.

What is so interesting is that NONE of the foods listed were made, caught, or grown domestically. The bread might be imported each day from Canada, the fish from Korea, and the fruit from North Africa. Each item would have been "processed" in various ways in order to have a longer shelf life and to travel well, and yet that family would say that they eat a very "natural" diet.

(Don't forget the "costs" of this sort of natural diet where the environment is concerned. All of the water, pesticides, and fuels used to catch, grow, make, and transport/distribute those foods are serious issues to consider too!)

So, that shows us that there is indeed a distinct difference between what we perceive as processed and natural, and the actual reality of the situation.

Why Processing Matters

By now you might be asking why any of this even matters. The answer is fairly simple: handling and processing reduces the value of the food.

Take that box of clementines from North Africa as an example. The fruits are:

1. Picked before fully ripe,
2. Gassed to ensure that they ripen at the right pace for marketability;
3. Irradiated or processed to reduce infestations or mold growth;
4. Shipped, and distributed via several forms of transport; and
5. This means that the nutritional content of the fruit has been degraded by all of that handling and/or processing.

Now, that is a "whole food," and things get far, far worse when we talk about a food that has to be processed in order to be created - like the bread mentioned above.

In that example, the food can be something made of wheat that has been milled and which has had its outer bran removed (meaning that very little nutrition exists in the grains or the flour that is made with them). The rest of the ingredients might not even be whole foods at all but instead a series of chemical blends that create a tasty loaf of bread. The end result, however, could be a product that is calorie laden and nutritionally void.

So, you could be eating processed foods and thinking that you are eating healthily. This is only one effect of processing and moving away from raw foods.

## The Impacts of Handling and Processing

Among the worst things that processing and handling food will do are:
- Killing natural "flora";
- Destroying enzymes;
- Changing the pH of the foods;
- Destroying the vitamins;
- Converting minerals into inorganic compounds; and
- Changing the food from "living" to "dead".

Let's take some time to explore each of these issues...

**Beneficial Flora**

Earlier we mentioned the material referred to as "intestinal flora". Many food scientists and nutritional experts agree that we each need our own "native" flora to keep our digestion healthy.

This means that most of us grow up in a relatively fixed area and are exposed to local or native bacteria, yeast, and even some parasites that become part of our own digestive system. This enables us to easily eat the local foods and get the most nutritional benefits from them. This is also why travelers who drink water in a foreign land might become ill from it - they are not acclimated to the native bacteria, etc.

Interestingly enough, the presence of this local flora begins during birth. Most children actually absorb some of these bacteria as they pass through the birth canal. They then receive another dose from their mother's breast milk. Unfortunately, almost everyone is exposed to things like antibiotics and a processed diet by the age of six months - which disrupts the natural development of your "gut flora". Thus, almost anyone can develop problems because of the lack of such useful materials.

Just consider that beneficial flora:

- Coat the digestive tract to act as a barrier between the blood stream and toxins;

- Prevent "leaky gut syndrome" from occurring (a condition that allows the intestinal walls to become porous and let harmful materials into the blood stream;
- Provide the probiotic microbes that produce enzymes essential to transporting minerals and vitamins through the intestinal walls;
- Chelate heavy metals, toxins, and carcinogens in order to allow us to safely excrete them from the body;
- Synthesize Vitamins K and B as well as the Amino Acids; and
- Create the foundation for a good immune system. They control pathogenic microbes and keep everything in balance. People who have "disbacteriosis" (who have lost native flora in their digestive tract) are far more prone to:
  - Acne, psoriasis, eczema, and skin conditions related to allergies;
  - Asthma;
  - Food allergies and seasonal allergies;
  - Irregular bowels; and
  - General illness due to a compromised immune system.

When we process foods, it tends to begin with washing them to the point that most native bacteria are destroyed. This is unfortunate because, as Dr. Ben Kim tells us in his article "The Importance of Friendly Intestinal Bacteria":

*"An excellent source of friendly bacteria is healthy soil. We are exposed to countless species of friendly bacteria when we are outdoors, playing and working in relatively unpolluted areas. Gardening and hiking in the woods are two of the best ways of exposing yourself to friendly bacteria on a regular basis. In fact, the best probiotic (friendly intestinal bacteria) supplements that I know of were originally created with strains of bacteria that were found in healthy soil."*

So, not only does taking a "hands off" approach to our food supply reduce our chances of getting beneficial bacteria, but processing tends to also eliminate it as well.

Okay, so we can see that modern, processed food will not provide us with essential intestinal flora and that their nutrition levels are lower because of the many things done to them, including heating and irradiating.

What we also have to realize is that raw food has most of the enzymes destroyed too.

## Enzymes and Modern Food

As we already stated - enzymes are huge where the raw diet is concerned. We already learned a bit about eating and digestion, but let's be sure we really understand enzymes.

## Enzymes 101

There are 45 "essential" nutrients that the human body needs if it will continue to function properly. They are not made or synthesized internally. This means that the body does not make them but must get them from outside sources, i.e. food.

These nutrients will include the vitamins and minerals that most people are familiar with, but also include water, fats, proteins, and carbohydrates too.

When food sources for nutrients are consumed they are then digested. As we know, digestion is when food is broken down and the nutrient contents are distributed to the cells, bloodstream, and organs. Because this happens at the molecular level we tend to take it for granted, but our bodies are amazing at directing the nutrients found in food to other nutrients, and creating chemical reactions that ensure the body functions.

Guess what controls this remarkable chain of processes? Enzymes.

Every single part of the digestive and metabolic process is initiated, managed, and brought to an end by a range of different enzymes. Without enzymes in our bodies and foods, our metabolism fails. This is actually something that can go on inside of a living human body, but it will be the body of a person who is not enjoying a healthy life.

Earlier we reviewed the various enzymes, but let's look at them in simple "umbrella" categories for now. They are:

- Food enzymes - within the food we eat are all of the enzymes needed to digest that particular food. When the food is heated, the enzymes are "denatured" or inactivated and will no longer help with digestion. This means that the work of breaking down the food and pulling out any nutrients goes to the digestive enzymes made inside of the body;

- Digestive enzymes - these are created by the bodily organs (though that makes them part of the metabolic enzymes, they are entirely unique because their only function is to digest the foods we eat). Digestive enzymes come strictly from digestive organs such as the salivary glands, the pancreas, the stomach, and the small intestine;

- Metabolic enzymes - these actually operate the body and live inside of the cells. They help to create new cells and maintain all of the bodily tissue. Every organ has special enzymes that know intuitively how to operate their respective systems and organs. These are the end process enzymes and will not actually break down food.

Now, that looks like an ideal and perfectly balanced system, but the trouble is that most people start by cooking their foods.

We understand that this kills off most of the natural food enzymes, and this means that the body's digestive enzymes must tackle the work. The more we demand that these enzymes break down and synthesize foods, the more strain we actually put on the entire body.

For example, one of the things you will learn is that the immune system can suffer when the diet is overly processed. This is because the organs and bodily systems working to digest food cannot then have the time or opportunity to rebuild/replace cells or tissue, and this means immunity suffers.

Just consider it a matter of priorities: your body's first priority is always going to be getting enough nutrition to function. This means it puts its major energies towards digesting and converting whatever food is available. When foods are processed (cooked), it means that the body is being asked to make all of the required enzymes, and this means things go easily out of balance.

What happens? There are two things that happen when we demand so much from the body where digestion and the creation of digestive enzymes are concerned:

1.  We deplete the body of its natural amounts of digestive enzymes and this disables us from fighting off disease and illness; and

2.  Our overworked bodies cannot make enough digestive enzymes and this allows undigested food into the body. This is like pollution and continually increases the risks for chronic disease.

Enzymes and Food Processing

So, what you have just learned is very important: processing foods reduces their nutrient levels AND tends to destroy most (if not all) of their natural food enzyme content.

Because food enzymes make food easily digestible in the human gut, the loss of them has profound and long lasting effects on the body. Without them, our bodies have to create or supplement from within. This stresses the digestive system and all associated organs, and eventually costs the entire body.

## Cooking Changes pH

Here is one of the most interesting problems with cooked and processed food: it ends up acidifying foods.

Now, that might make you think that it leads to higher use of antacids such as Tums, etc. That is not really what we mean.

The pH scale of the human body is usually defined as a measurement of the amount of oxygen in your blood. Get too acidic and the blood is unable to carry enough oxygen to the cells, get too alkaline and it transports too much.

So, just like the baby bear in "Goldilocks and the Three Bears," you have to try to keep your pH levels "just right". That means a measure of around 7 to 7.45.

When levels are too low - meaning acidic - you will be tired, irritable, sleep badly, feel sensitive to the cold, and be prone to illness. People who are chronically or perpetually acidic are often going to have such long term problems as Cancer, Arthritis, and allergies.

Take a guess at one of the primary ways of making the body "just right"...yes, through the diet!

The body always tries to neutralize any problems in the pH by eliminating acids from the body via sweat, breath, urine, or even storing them as fat. The body will also pull alkaline materials from foods to help with balance issues.

This means that one of the best ways to keep your body's pH under control is to eat foods that are raw, i.e. not acidic, or which are naturally alkalizing.

This is confusing to many because they think of acidic foods, such as lemon, and avoid it. This is unfortunate because many raw foods that seem acidic are actually great alkaline food sources - that lemon is just one example. Generally, however, when someone eats a "balanced" raw diet they get the right amounts of both alkaline and acid. (We provide a list of alkaline foods in the last chapter)

For instance, a single meal will give them the plant based calcium, silica, sodium, magnesium and potassium they need to remain in balance.

## Destroys the Vitamins

When discussing vitamin loss from cooking it is imperative to begin with a look at "water soluble" vitamins. Why? In the human body there are water soluble and fat soluble vitamins. The fat soluble vitamins are stored in adipose (fat) tissue and used when needed. This is why supplementation is not always needed.

The water soluble vitamins, on the other hand, dissolve in the water in the human body, and are not stored in any way. Whatever is not metabolized by the body is passed out through the urine.

This means that a diet low in certain water soluble vitamins may be made even lower if the individual also cooks their food sources. Nowhere is this more obvious than with the water soluble vitamins C and the B-complexes. Though the body needs only small amounts, they are made unstable when heated, and this means that you may not be getting them.

Why is that important? Just consider the vitamin B complexes; they include: vitamin B-6, vitamin B-12, folate, thiamin, riboflavin, niacin, biotin and pantothenic acid. These materials are responsible for everything from good vision and skin to a good appetite and a healthy nervous system. Depleting the body of them on a regular basis is going to eventually take its toll.

The lack of Vitamin C is a major issue of concern as well as this is going to impact oral health, bone and cartilage health, and even absorption of other minerals and vitamins.

We don't recommend that you consider supplements as a solution to nutrient loss in some foods. Although you are avoiding cooking your foods, and preserving nutrients, your body can only take the materials that it needs at the exact times it needs it.

So, you can swallow a lot of vitamin capsules each morning, but your body may not pull the nutrients from them because you may not need them at the time. Instead of artificial supplements, you should aim to give your body a better chance at getting the nutrition it requires through whole food sources. This is an optimized delivery system that the body can manage much more efficiently, and is best done through a balanced diet that is consumed over the course of each day.

Minerals into Inorganic Compounds

Cooking doesn't just destroy vitamins, however. It can also cause chemical changes that convert organic materials into "inorganic" ones (meaning that the carbon has been removed). That alone is not necessarily a bad thing because the human body already contains both organic and inorganic minerals.

Just consider:

- Organic minerals in the body = amino acids, sulfur, iron, etc.

- Inorganic minerals in the body =sodium chloride

So, why should it matter if food is converted by cooking in this way? It is because it makes the minerals even more difficult to assimilate.

We have already discovered that food sources of a mineral such as calcium are ideal for balancing the pH, but when that calcium is overheated and converted into an inorganic mineral, it can make it too difficult for the body to metabolize.

This means that organic minerals are:

- Much easier to digest,
- Make your body more alkaline, and
- Are far more beneficial.

Always keep in mind that the body's priority is to digest food to the fullest degree possible, and to get adequate nutrition. Forcing it to handle inorganic minerals is only making the body's work even harder. This opens you up to a host of problems, the least of which is an imbalanced pH.

**Changes from Living to Dead**

Cook some beans, put them in some soil and see what happens. Yes, they rot. Leave them in their natural and uncooked state and put them into that same soil and watch. Yes, they create life. They can sprout and use energy. This means that uncooked food has life potential while cooked food has only rot potential.

While that may seem like a harsh illustration, it is fundamentally true. You can take almost any sort of uncooked whole food (naturally raw dairy is the exception) and see how it can still "live". Tops of carrots, wilted potatoes, apple seeds, avocado pits...they all have the life potential or the life force inside of them. This provides a profoundly nourishing sort of energy to those who eat such foods.

AGE

Lastly, the cooking process creates something known as AGE or advanced glycation products. These are potentially harmful compounds that can actually lead cells to age quickly.

When you eat a raw food diet it always has the potential of slowing the aging process and also reducing inflammation and cellular disruption.

## Making the Change

After reading all of these things it is likely that you are thinking of a raw food diet for yourself or your family. That is great, but don't jump in without full knowledge. In the next chapter we look at all of the facts and even hear a bit about what those opposed to this way of eating feel.

# CHAPTER THREE

## A Raw Diet Explained

*"Depending on the source, a raw food diet is either a path to perfect health or to serious undernourishment. The truth is somewhere in the middle. Devotees insist that a diet consisting mainly of uncooked, unprocessed plant foods leads to a leaner body, clearer skin, and higher energy. They also believe it cuts the risk of disease."*

(From "Raw Food Diet Review" at WebMD.com)

Now that you understand what happens when foods are cooked and processed and how modern dietary choices might negatively impact our bodies, we can begin to focus almost entirely on raw food eating.

For example, the typical raw foodist will tend to use the following techniques on a daily basis:

- Soaking and sprouting
- Sprouting
- Dehydrating
- Blending
- Juicing
- Fermenting
- Pickling
- Chopping and slicing

This list already shows that the raw diet is not all about crunching on a whole apple or eating a big pile of lettuce. Instead, it will involve various textures and processes meant to allow for optimal health while delivering appealing and flavorful foods. For example, we provide a killer recipe for French Fries (Yes, French Fries!) in the final chapter.

Just consider that a raw food advocate will have some juices and/or smoothies each day, some cold soups, chopped salads, and even sandwiches that use whole foods rather than baked goods. They are going to also get food at the "peak" of freshness and this means optimal flavor too.

**Breaking Down the Diet**

What you will find when you begin looking through eating plans and recommendations for a raw diet is that:

- 75% of the diet is made up of fruits and vegetables;
- 25% of the diet is made of germinated seeds, nuts, and can even contain raw animal products too;
- 10% of calories come from fat; and
- 25g or less protein is consumed each day.

Anyone considering the shift to a raw food diet is encouraged to do a basic assessment of their calorie needs and to determine the most appropriate goals for their health. For example, the person with diabetes needs to consider the right choices, etc. (A free diet assessment tool is available online at FitDay.com and will also help with nutrient levels too!)

Always keep in mind that a raw food diet translates to high volume. You must be prepared to eat pounds of food each day if you want to take in the necessary calories and nutrients. Because the diet is going to provide plenty of carbohydrates, protein, and fat when done correctly it is necessary to really customize accordingly.

This is true of any diet, but those opposing the raw diet tend to say that lack of adequate nutrition is one of the negatives of this way of life. This is a bit unfair, but we'll look at what they say and respond in the next section.

The things to keep in mind are:

1. The raw diet can be completely customized to meet your dietary needs;
2. Raw eating allows for a tremendous range of variety;
3. A lot of volume is required when using a 100% raw diet;
4. The primarily vegetarian aspect of the raw diet can reduce high cholesterol and lower glucose levels too;
5. There are many techniques used in the making of raw foods and meals;
6. The raw diet provides living food sources;
7. The raw diet is high in fiber and this means it is great for cleansing the body;
8. The raw diet is capable of helping the body to fight disease and infection;
9. The raw diet is safe for anyone with any sort of health condition if they create a plan based on their needs;
10. The raw diet can be used for weight loss, by vegans or vegetarians, for children, for those who want to "detoxify" their bodies and eliminate bad food cravings, and by those with pH issues; and
11. MOST IMPORTANTLY - the raw food diet can be either 100% raw, or qualifies when it is around 75% raw foods mixed with 25% cooked foods.

These facts are important to know when you start to read anything written by those opposed to a raw food diet.

Why? Most anti-raw foodists insist that this is an "extreme" way of eating and yet do not issue the same criticisms of diets that eliminate entire food groups such as "carbs" or most fruits, etc.

Let's take some time now to see what the "opposition" has to say in order to understand their concerns.

**The Opposition**

So, to get right into the debate, let's look at many of the most common concerns provided by those opposed to raw diets:

- Food poisoning - While concerns about food poisoning are valid, the list of "concerns" includes:
  - Some saying that cooking food below 118 degrees Fahrenheit may not kill food-borne pathogens.
  - Others point out that raw or undercooked animal products can be very risky.
  - Still more point to the major issues with many kinds of raw produce since the 70s and how outbreaks of E-Coli and Salmonella are common.

- Deficiencies - One of the loudest of complaints against the raw diet is the lack of certain nutrients. Common complains say:
    o There are ANF or antinutrient factors in raw foods that cooking can destroy.
    o Kids may not get enough calories, fatty and amino acids, and vitamins from a vegan and raw diet.
    o There are some who point to Vitamin B12 (found mostly in animal products) deficiency, and how it can lead to anemia and neurological problems.
    o Some experts warn of Lycopene deficiency which is most abundant in cooked tomatoes., and
    o Others point out the rise of amenorrhoea (lack of menstruation due to being under or overweight) in raw foodists.
- Less nutritious - There are some who point out that specific kinds of nutrients are enhanced by cooking. For example, some compounds in broccoli are improved by cooking. Also, foods such as eggs and tomatoes are better for the body if they are cooked.

- Time - many argue that preparing raw foods is always going to demand substantially more time than traditional modern food preparation.
- Cost - Many insist that a diet packed with fresh vegetables and raw food sources is going to be far more detrimental to the budget than the average diet.

While we do have to say that there are some valid "cons" listed above, for the most part they are not that valid. Most of them are the product of a lack of adequate information or even misinformation. We'll take the time to look at them on a point by point basis below.

The Responses

- Food poisoning
    - Yes, the lack of heat can mean that foodborne pathogens are not killed, but let's not isolate the risks only to raw foodists! The recalls on contaminated foods go nationwide and impact everyone who is eating them. Consider too that many raw foodists "buy locally" to get organic and optimal foods, which mean that many actually avoid the contaminations and potential pathogen issues!
    - Animal products are not always a huge component of a true raw foodist. Though

there are vegans and vegetarians, there are also some that opt to eat raw eggs and even fish or beef. The USDA is now exploring methods of ensuring safety in the raw dairy supply because so many consumers in general want untreated milk, cheese, etc. The use of antibiotics, hormones, and other potentially harmful substances in the raising of livestock has led to this, and it is not raw foodists alone that have triggered such widespread action. Keep in mind that many raw food advocates also buy raw milk from local sources and understand the cleanliness and health of the farm animals.

- Deficiencies
  - ANF - The risks of any ANF are canceled by the presence of pure vitamin and mineral sources. If a food has a compound that inhibits nutrient absorption, the volume and balance of any raw diet will quickly outweigh or counteract this problem.
  - Kids – some worry about inadequate nutrition on this diet. The reality is that

many balanced raw diets have to be careful about protein levels because they give too much. Additionally, the stress and strain of digesting and metabolizing cooked foods is removed from the children's bodies, and this means that they can actually get the most from every meal because all of their energy is freed to do what is necessary.

o General vitamin and mineral deficiencies - if you follow the advice of raw food experts, you create an organized optimal eating plan that ensures you get all that you need. This not only remedies any worries about deficiency, but also means you get plenty of calories too.

- Less nutritious - there is a fantastic, and remarkably lengthy, study available online at BeyondVeg.com. It is called "Does Cooking Render Minerals 'Inorganic' or Less Assimiable" and it has some terrific data. The quotes below are particularly relevant where nutrition in raw food is concerned:

*"First, virtually all foods contain more nutrients in the raw state...The nutritiousness of a given food may or may not be improved by cooking, or only by certain*

*methods of cooking. There may be an ideal temperature, or an ideal cooking time...Finally, to put cooking in a broader perspective, many other processing techniques have been used by humans to improve digestibility, such as soaking, sprouting, fermentation, aging, leaching of toxins and antinutrients, acid or alkaline treatment, etc. Cooking is sometimes helpful--overdoing it isn't. Obviously, whenever a food can be eaten raw with better results, it is preferable to do so and to be recommended."*

- Time - It takes no more or less time to whip up a raw meal (including smoothies, "sandwiches", soups, etc.) than it does to create an out of the box/freezer/microwave meal. In fact, some raw foodists find that they spend much less time because they rarely peel, chop, and cook things any longer.

- Cost - The most expensive items at the grocery store are rarely going to be the foods eaten raw. Think of the price of a big piece of red meat or that cake from the bakery. Per serving, those foods are far more expensive than seasonal fruits and vegetables, seeds and nuts, and fresh raw dairy items.

Generally, you can see that few of the "cons" that are so often pointed out by those opposed to the raw food diet are accurate.

Because we didn't touch on all of the "myths" associated with raw eating, let's close out this chapter by debunking some of the very worst of them. This will ensure you see the benefits of changing your diet and will get you very excited about the last chapter, which shows you how to start following your own raw diet plans!

**Debunking the Raw Food Myths**

1. Cold Food Forever - does the thought of room temperature or cold foods for the rest of your life make you want to cry? While a scalding bowl of soup is out of the question, don't forget that raw foodists have a fixed temperature in mind. This means that they do accept the heating of foods.

For example, you can heat a bit of puree to 104 degrees if you want to take the edge off of it straight out of the refrigerator. You can even use a food dehydrator to bring them to a controlled temperature too. This might be nice for a green salad that will benefit from that "wilted" texture, etc. Don't forget that hot tea and beverages are always acceptable too! (If you are doing less than 100% raw you can also enjoy those foods heated and/or cooked each day as well)

2. All Raw - we've already touched on this, but will do so a few more times. You don't have to go

100% raw to get the benefits of this diet. The experts say that "mostly raw" (generally meaning from 75% to 95% as optimal levels) is just as beneficial.

Now, don't take this to mean that you can suddenly eat 25% junk and processed and not cancel out the raw choices, because it doesn't mean that at all. Instead, go for unprocessed, organic, and "whole food" sources.

3. Never Dining Out - don't think that you have no options for restaurant dining if you are a raw foodist! Big cities now have many award winning "raw" restaurants. You can also choose a vegan or vegetarian restaurant and find plenty of choices as well. Consider too that you can easily find smoothies, salads, and more when dining out.

4. Only fruits and veggies - this has been one of the biggest myths around and is just plain silly. The truly raw diet does use fruits and vegetables (around 75% of the daily diet consists of them) but also has nuts, sprouted grains, fermented foods, oils of many kinds, nut milks, juices, and so much more! In fact, the "breakdown" includes:

   a. Green leafy vegetables (preference is given to them over all other types of vegetables because chlorophyll foods are essential to body functions, and because of their immense nutrient and oxygen contents);

b. Sugary fruits (citrus, mangoes and melons are ideal);

c. Fatty foods (avocados, olives, nuts, and seeds are ideal)

Keep in mind that a 100% raw diet also equals a high volume of food.

For instance, the average female is supposed to eat around six pounds of fruit, two and a half pounds of vegetables, and around 1/4 of a pound of nuts or seeds each day. The average man is supposed to take in around seven and half pounds of fruit, three pounds of vegetables, and around .33 pounds of nuts and seeds. That is a lot, and is the reason that things like purees and smoothies come in so handy.

5. Living in the kitchen - this is another one already touched on, but you have to understand how inaccurate it is! We already listed the ways that raw foods are "made", and the list included blending, dehydrating, fermenting, etc. This means that your blender is probably going to become your favorite tool, but it also shows that

you may simply need to wash, coarsely chop, and purée foods to get a fast and nutrient rich meal!

Okay, you now have all of the arguments in favor of a raw diet...let's start to learn how to cook and live on raw foods and beverages.

## Chapter Four

---

### Adding Raw Foods to Your Diet

Don't, and we really mean DO NOT, just jump into the raw diet. If you are living even a reasonably healthy diet it is going to be extremely uncomfortable to start eating only raw foods.

Why? Well, the bulky fiber in these foods is going to take a bit of time to get yourself used to. If you suddenly start feeding yourself raw fruits, vegetables, nuts and beans you are going to be extremely bloated and gassy. Your body is not going to be ready for it. So, that means you need to follow a transitional plan.

Not only does the transitional period let your body get used to more fiber, but it also allows you to start drinking more water (which helps digestion), and getting "unhooked" from your processed food addictions. These processed foods tend to include: sugar, salt, flour, sweeteners, baked goods, fats, meats, pastas, dairy, and candies (among others).

## Making the Switch

Below is a list of options that can help the modern eater shift comfortably into a raw diet. We suggest that you try to make the change over the course of two weeks or less as the longer you hold on to your original food patterns the longer it takes for your body to begin benefiting from this new way of life.

Transitional Tips and Pointers

Before we list the most common food addictions and how to overcome them, we'd like to give some very general and useful pointers. They are:

1. Meat - begin by cutting the red meats, pork, chicken, and then fish. If you are going to be mostly raw, you can safely keep the fish in the diet without any sort of problematic issues, just make sure you don't eat fish with high mercury levels. Salmon is always a good healthy choice that usually has low levels of mercury.

2. Cooked - we don't suggest anything more than 25% cooked food each day. Optimally you would want around 5% to 10% instead. If you do keep cooked foods in the diet, eat only one type at any

time, combine it with a vegetable juice or a large salad, and eat it only at the end of the day.

3. Substitute don't Starve - you are already challenging yourself by opting to go raw. Don't make things even more difficult by totally eliminating favorites. Instead, make a pointed effort to find raw substitutes that satisfy your cravings. Also, don't let go of everything at once. Pick one major issue to alleviate, such as pasta, and not pasta and red meat in the same week.

4. Do breakfast first - it is easiest if you start the transition with breakfast only. This is a very easy time to begin using smoothies of all kinds and adding the most important raw compounds such as the greens and oils essential to a healthy raw lifestyle.

5. Get ready! - a lot of people struggle initially with raw food efforts because they didn't discover the kinds of options and substitutes they had available. For example, we recommend that you:

   a. Find resources - raw health food stores, online distributors, and groups offering raw foods are great for getting odd ingredients and answers to questions.

   b. Condiments - you will have cravings or miss certain foods. The most successful raw foodists are those who kept sea salt, lemon juice, cider vinegar, and oils handy. This is because these are great for giving you the "zing" you crave without getting you off of the raw diet. Don't forget the sesame seeds for calcium and the hemp seeds for protein and crunch!

   c. Nutritional yeast - if you are going 100% raw you might struggle with Vitamin B12. Sprinkling zesty nutritional yeast on foods will automatically give you the nutrient you are missing and make the food even more flavorful!

6. Fill the Pantry - the raw foodist has to eat a lot and will need some special ingredients too. Below is our list of "must have items" (in addition to the fruits, vegetables, and any animal products you intend to use) that will help you get off to the best start:

   a. Nuts and Seeds - these should be raw, dried, and organic:

      i.      Almonds

      ii.     Brazil nuts

      iii.    Cashews

      iv.    Chia seeds

      v.     Flax seeds

      vi.       Hemp seeds

      vii.     Macadamia nuts

      viii.    Pine nuts

      ix.       Pumpkin seeds

      x.        Raw nut butters

      xi.       Sesame seeds

      xii.     Sunflower seeds

      xiii.    Tahini

b.  Grains - raw and organic are best:

      i.        Buckwheat

      ii.       Millet

      iii.     Oats

      iv.      Quinoa

      v.       Spelt flour

c.  Beans - meant for sprouting, will include organic:

      i.        Adzuki

      ii.       Chickpeas

      iii.     Mung

      iv.      Lentils

d.  Oils

      i.        Chia oil

      ii.       Cold pressed extra virgin olive oil

      iii.     Raw coconut butter and raw coconut oil

        iv.        Herbs/spices/condiments

        v.         Raw apple cider

        vi.        Cayenne pepper

        vii.       Celtic sea salt

        viii.     Cinnamon

        ix.        Cumin

        x.         Curry

        xi.        Dill

        xii.       Raw Soy Sauce

        xiii.     Raw Honey

        xiv.     Raw vanilla beans

        xv.       Seaweeds

        xvi.     Sundried tomatoes

e. Raw vinegars

f. Sweetening

        i.         Raw  honey

        ii.        Agave nectar

        iii.      Coconut nectar

        iv.       Stevia

        v.         Date sugar

        vi.        Yacon

g. Etc.

        i.         Tapenade

        ii.        Black olives

        iii.      Soy

        iv.       Unpasteurized miso

      v. Herbal teas

      vi.     Carob powder

      vii.    Raw cacao nibs

      viii.   Fermented items such as miso, kimchee, sauerkraut

      ix.     Goji berries

      x.      Maca powder

      xi.     Bee pollen

      xii.    Spirulina

7. Kitchen Prep - you will also want to have the following devices available for use in your kitchen each day too:

    a. Juicer

    b. Blender

    c. Dehydrator

    d. Food processor

    e. Coffee grounder

    f. Sprouter

    g. Good knives and cutting boards

    h. Glass storage jars for leftover juices, ingredients, etc.

## Getting Started

Once you are ready to begin, you want to consider how to eliminate your biggest food problems. We have not mentioned the term SAD yet because we did not want the focus to be on the modern diet, but SAD is the acronym for Standard American Diet.

This is one that is packed with processed foods, and you are probably someone who follows that SAD. So, you will need to shake the habit, and the best tactic is to identify the components of that diet that you are particularly fond of or addicted to. So, below we provide great foods to use to transition away from the SAD ones and over to the healthier raw versions.

- Sugar - in the SAD world this category includes corn syrup, malt, dextrose, and rice syrup. You will want to turn to raw fruits as a primary source of "sweetness" in the diet, but you can use stevia, raw honey, and coconut too.
- Salt - iodized salt, table salt, and any artificial sodium flavor enhancers are a big "no no". Instead, go for unrefined sea salt, seaweed, and even celery.
- Flour - processed to death are any wheat, corn, or rice flours. Even lesser evils such as spelt flour, buckwheat flour, and brown rice flour are not so good. If you miss the flour from a recipe, try sprouted grains, coconut flour, or almond flour as good substitutions.

- Sweeteners - see sugar substitutes above (and be sure that you are getting rid of aspartame, splenda, xylitol and the rest of the fake sugars).

- Baked goods - bread, cakes, cookies and any of the other high fat and calorie foods made from flour have to go. Not only do they take a lot of energy to digest but they are also nutritionally void and prone to spiking blood sugar. Instead, replace these with any raw desserts, raw fruits, and "wraps" made from leafy greens.

- Fats - butter, lard, shortening, margarine, and any other sort of fat is best replaced by cold pressed olive or coconut oil, flax or hemp seed oil, or the optimal choices of whole food sources such as nuts, fresh coconut, seeds, etc.

- Meats - any animal meats, including bacon or cold cuts should be eliminated. You can have organic raised, nitrate free, and no-MSG meats, but it is best to use raw recipes for vegan meat substitutes such as "pate" or "meatballs" made from seeds, nuts, etc. Fish is a bit different, and you can eat wild fish or cold smoked fish without concerns about loss of nutrients, but just be wary of mercury levels.

- Pastas - very hard to shake, pasta is a staple of many SADs. The only suggested raw substitute is raw spaghetti squash that has been "heated" to less than 104 degrees.

- Dairy - any cheese, milk, yogurt, or other dairy foods should be eliminated if you are going vegan and raw. If not, you can use organic raw goat or sheep's milks and cheeses, or you can seek to find reliable sources of organic milk as well. Optimally, you would replace all of these with calcium rich nut or seed "cheeses", raw almond milk or milk made with other nuts, raw coconut milk, and kefir.

- Eggs - leave behind regular eggs and opt for organic and free range eggs. To reduce contamination risks when using eggs in recipes, replace them with agar agar or flax seed.

- Condiments - this is another challenging area for many people transitioning into a raw diet. Fortunately, you can make some great substitutes without cooking any of the ingredients. Consider such foods as ketchup, mayonnaise, salad dressing, pasta sauce, and spreads for bread can all be made with entirely raw ingredients. We give recipes for most below!

## Eating Plans

Okay, so you have some of the best transitional tips and you know which items to put into the pantry. Now, how do you go about eating a raw diet? As we suggested, the best plan is to make a slow shift (usually over the course of two weeks or more) with a single meal being replaced as the first step.

So, a recommended eating plan would look like this:

- Days One through Three: Only change to the diet is a raw breakfast. We suggest a smoothie or shake.
- Days Four through Six: Raw breakfast, with all snacks being replaced by raw options.
- Days Seven through Nine: Replace lunch with raw choices.
- Days Ten through Thirteen: Remove all meat sources from the daily diet, and now have only raw dinners.
- Days Fourteen and onward: Continue to refine the diet and adjust accordingly.

See how easy it might be? Of course, everyone is different in terms of what they need to get from their diet. So, you will have to stop and actually "map out" what you intend to eat. Unlike SADs, you cannot just rely on some "instant fix" if you are in need of a meal. You have to be sure you are getting all of the nutrients in a balanced way. As you have learned, it is not that complicated a thing to do, but you do need to get your RDA (Recommended Daily Allowance) and be sure you are meeting all of your nutritional needs. A good table of RDA amounts is available here: http://en.wikipedia.org/wiki/Reference_Daily_Intake

Remember, however, that if you are removing meat from the diet to begin with the red meats and work your way to fish, etc.

Remember too that you want to pay attention to calorie needs, nutrition levels (especially B12 if you are going 100%) and being sure to drink enough water to help with detoxification.

Keep in mind that chewing is essential too! One of the main errors made by those transitioning into this way of eating is to chew only to their normal levels when it is necessary that they masticate a great deal more than normal.

If you're aiming for 75% raw – try to eat an all-raw breakfast and make sure that 75% of your plate is raw for your other meals.

# Recipes

Now you can begin to see how to eat like a true raw foodist. You are going to be remarkably stimulated by the "palette" of foods you have available, and you should be sure that you experiment and have fun.

### Smoothies and Juices

### Smoothie Basics

This is a raw diet staple, and requires only that you seek to create the flavors and textures you desire. You can make sweet or savory smoothies, and one of the most common that you will see is the "Green Smoothie". We give you a good version of that below too!

**Basic Recipe and Steps:**

1. Wash the vegetables and fruits.

2. Pre-cut the vegetables.
3. Put food with the highest water content in the bottom of the blender first.
4. Add enough water for blending - covering with water. If you don't use enough water, the ingredients don't blend well.
5. Blend until really smooth, but not so long that the fluid gets warm.
6. Serve and drink immediately.

## Green Smoothie

1 Avocado

1 Whole Peeled Orange

1 Banana Peeled

1 Stalk Celery

1/2 Apple

1 teaspoon Super Greens Powder (you can find many versions of this product and each is basically just a raw plant based protein powder)

*Add to blender and mix until smooth.*

## World's Best Smoothie

1 teaspoon of raw carob powder (or raw chocolate)

1 tablespoon goji berries

1/2 teaspoon maca powder

1 teaspoon bee pollen

1 tablespoon hemp seed

1 teaspoon raw honey (or yakon root or few drops stevia)

1 teaspoon green powder (spirulina, chlorella, wheatgrass)

Few Leafs Of Greens (Such As Spinach Or Dandelion)

Few Scoops Of Coconut Meat (Optional)

2 cups special warm herb tea or pure water or coconut water

*Blend as directed, and enjoy!*

## Savory Smoothie

5 leafs of red leaf lettuce

1/2 avocado

2 stalks celery

Juice of 1/2 lemon

5 stalks parsley or cilantro

2 cups water

*Blend as directed, and enjoy!*

## Super Sweet Mango Smoothie

1 mango - peeled, pitted and cut into chunks

2 bananas - peeled and sliced

1-2 oranges peeled and broken into slices

Dash of lemon juice

1 tablespoon hemp seed

1/4 teaspoon green powder

Ice cubes (optional)

*Put all ingredients in the blender and add a bit of water if the mixture is too thick.*

## Summerific Peach Smoothie

Use any stone fruit, or even pears if you like.

2 peaches (pitted)

Meat from about 1 young coconut (about 1/2 cup)

2 cups coconut water

Ice cubes (optional)

*Open the coconut and pour the water in the blender jar. Scoop out the meat with a spoon. Put all ingredients in the blender and blend well. You can replace the coconut with 2.5 cups almond milk.*

## Crazy Simple Carrot Juice

2 pounds carrots

1/2 lemon

*Wash the lemon and cut most of the peel off. Juice the lemon and the carrots.*

Reliable Veggie Juice

3 cups chopped tomatoes

1 stalk celery

1 cucumber

3 drops stevia (optional)

1/2 teaspoon Himalayan sea salt

Pepper

Cayenne pepper

*Juice the tomatoes, celery, and cucumber in your juicer. Add drops stevia if you like a sweeter taste, and add the salt, pepper and cayenne pepper to taste. Adding a 1/4 onion, fresh oregano, and basil and red bell pepper are great additions too.*

## Breakfast Friendly Foods

## Oatmeal

What is breakfast without oatmeal and this is an amazingly good substitute for the SAD version.

2 apples

1 banana

1 tablespoon golden flax seed

2 teaspoons cinnamon

1/4 Water

*Put the flax seeds in the water and let sit overnight. Peel the apples and cut them in smaller parts. Peel the banana and slice. Rinse the flax seeds. Put everything in the blender. Add 1/4 cup water, and blend until smooth.*

*Make the recipe richer by replacing the water with almond milk. You may also add a tablespoon of hemp seeds, germinated nuts or raisins.*

## Yogurt

1/2 cup coconut water

1 cup coconut meat

1/2 teaspoon vanilla extract

*Open the coconut and pour the coconut water in the blender and some or all of the milk. Blend at high speed until it is the consistency of yogurt. Great with Granola*

## Rolled Energy Bars

1.5 cups dates (pitted)

1 cup nuts (i.e. raw cashews, almonds, pecans, or mix)

Pinch of salt

*Use a fork to mash the dates into a paste - using the blender is not often successful. Put the nuts into a food processor and process them almost to a powder but leave some chunks. Stir nuts into the dates and blend with your hands. Roll the mixture into a snake and cut into four lengths. Wrap in organic wax paper and store in the fridge.*

*You can also use figs, apricots, raisins, goji berries, dried apples and a combination of fruits and nuts. Try tossing some hemp or sesame seeds into the mix and even use some cinnamon, lemon juice, or vanilla for "zing".*

## Carob Nut Chews

3/4 cup raw walnuts, cashews or pecans

1/4 cup raw carob powder

1 cup raisins

*Process all ingredients in a food processor until sticky. Shape into balls and enjoy!*

*If you can't get the mixture to hold together, add a few more raisins and a tablespoon of water.*

## Lunchtime Favorites

## Wraps

We like to use lettuce or large spinach leaves to replace classic wraps. A basic recipe for this SAD sandwich substitute is:

1 carrot (cut into matchstick pieces)

1 ripe mango (peeled, seeded, cut into strips)

1/4 cup honey

1/2 cup lemon juice

1 1/2 tablespoon chopped ginger

1/2 tablespoon red chili

1 tablespoon soy sauce

1 cup raw almond butter

1/2 head savoy cabbage, shredded

6 very large spinach leaves or large romaine lettuce leaves ("Wraps")

1/2 cup hemp seed

1 handful cilantro

1 handful basil (torn)

Himalaya sea salt

*In a blender, puree the honey, lemon juice, ginger, red chili, and soy sauce. Add the almond butter and blend at low speed to combine. In a bowl, mix the almond butter dressing with the cabbage.*

*Create wraps by rolling the cabbage with dressing in a spinach or lettuce leaf. Add some hemp seeds, a few sticks of carrot, a few pieces of mango, and a few leafs of cilantro and, basil before rolling.*

## Raw Gazpacho

4 tomatoes, diced

1/2 medium white onion, diced

1 glove garlic, peeled and minced

Lemon juice to taste

1 cucumber, peeled and chopped

Toppings:

Freshly chopped cilantro

1 scallion (green part), finely chopped, for garnish

1 red bell pepper, seeded cored, and diced

1 table spoon raw virgin olive oil

1/4 cup mango, diced in small cubes

*Place all soup ingredients a blender and puree. Strain to remove any vegetable pieces and pits that are not fully liquefied. Chill overnight. Before serving, sprinkle the toppings you prefer.*

## Super Duper Cole Slaw

1 ripe mango, peeled and cut in small dice

1/2 head white cabbage, shredded

1/4 cup red cabbage, shredded

1/4 cup carrots, shredded

2 tablespoons honey or agave nectar (or 1 tbsp and few drops stevia)

1/2 cup lemon juice

2 tablespoons chopped ginger

1/2 tablespoon red chili

1 1/2 tablespoon tamari

1 cup raw almond or peanut butter

1/2 cup raw cashews

1 handful cilantro

1 handful torn basil

Himalaya sea salt

*In a blender, puree the honey, lemon juice, ginger, red chili and tamari. Add the raw almond butter and blend at low speed to combine. Add water to thin if necessary.*

*In a bowl mix the cabbage and the raw almond butter mixture. Add the raw cashews and mango pieces. Top with leafs of cilantro and basil and a few pieces of mango and or carrots for color.*

## Vegan Cheese

Spread this on cucumber slices, broil on top of tomatoes, or just use as a dip!

1 cup pine nuts (soaked in water for 2 hours)

1 tablespoon extra virgin olive oil

1 tablespoon lemon juice

1/2 teaspoon sea salt

1 glove garlic

Pepper

Fresh chives

*Put all ingredients - except the chives - in your blender or food processor. Blend until smooth. Snip the chives into the mixture and stir with fork.*

Salad Dressing

Simply combine:

- A raw plant fat

- With a sugar.

For example, you can blend half an avocado with an orange in the blender and pour that on your salad as a dressing. Just look at commercial salad dressings - they consist of two basic ingredients a fat and a sugar. Just make your own versions with raw ingredients!

## Mayonnaise

*Most raw foodists use avocado as a mayo replacement, but you can also find packaged versions made entirely with organic and raw ingredients. For example, you can find nut and seed versions made specifically for those following raw diets.*

*If you want the "from scratch" approach, you simply blend your seeded and peeled avocado with a small amount of lemon until smooth.*

## Dinner Friendly Recipes

## Best Dinner Salad

1 avocado, pitted
Juice of 1/2 lemon
1 tsp of whole grain mustard
few tbsp of pure water
1/2 head of white cabbage, shredded
1 carrot, shredded

*Blend the avocado, mustard, and lemon juice in the blender until smooth. Add water if needed. Put cabbage and carrots in a bowl and cover with dressing. Toss and serve.*

## Pasta Sauce

We make pasta by slicing zucchini or squash with a food peeler!

6 large tomatoes

5 sun dried tomatoes

2 garlic cloves

1/2 bunch fresh basil

2 tablespoons oregano

1 tablespoon freshly ground black pepper

1/4 cup onion, chopped

1/2 cup cold-pressed olive oil

1/4 cup lemon juice

4 dates, pitted

1 teaspoon Himalayan sea salt

*Put all ingredients in a blender and blend until creamy. Add water if you feel the consistency is too thick. Add toppings like olives, chopped tomatoes, onions or basil to give it an authentic flair.*

*You might also stir in some raw pesto too.*

## Pesto

1 bunch of parsley

2 bunches of basil

1/4 cup pine nuts

1/8 tsp Himalayan salt

1/4 cup olive oil (or more if required for smooth consistency)

*Put everything into the blender and puree until smooth.*

## French Fries with Ketchup

Fries

4 kohlrabi

1/2 cups cold pressed olive or hemp seed oil

2 teaspoons Curcumin

1 teaspoon sea salt

*Cut the kohlrabi into julienne strips using a mandoline or food processor. Put them in the bowl and pour the oil, Curcumin and salt over them. Toss to coat and let marinate for 30 minutes. Drain on a towel and remove excess oil. Serve with ketchup*

## Ketchup

3 tomatoes

3 sun dried tomatoes (soaked in water for two hours)

5 dates

1 squeeze lemon juice

1/2 cup pure water

*Put all ingredients in a blender. On the bottom of the blender the water, lemon juice and tomatoes, on top the dried tomatoes and dates. Blend well.*

Made in the USA
Monee, IL
01 February 2024